MW00878854

Everything
in
Between

Dedication

To Matthew and Ronan, my brothers without whom I would be lost.

Stay Updated on My Work
Follow Me:

Instagram: @authortravisliebert

Tumblr: @authortravisliebert

Check out my other books

This is Death, Love, Life

Perchance to Dream

Contents:

Forever is a myth we created
A fiction we made
Just so we could survive ourselves
But lying here tangled up with you
Feeling your breath on my neck
It seems forever is only a kiss away

     -Forever

I have always been
A hopeless romantic
Tripping over my heart
And falling in love with anyone
Who spared a glance in my direction
But no matter how long
I glance into the mirror
I have never been able
To love myself
   -Hopeless Romantic

An invitation to sin
With lips to tempt the devil
Baptize me in your kisses
Feed me the Eucharist of your skin
Hold me in the sweet embrace of your allure
    -Invitation to Sin

I stroll through gardens beheading roses
And bring home bundles of thorny green stems
Then place them in vases and wonder why they
wither and die
Was my love not enough?
They pricked my hands, wounded me and drew
my blood
And yet I loved them
And yet it wasn't enough
I know good things never last
But what about the bad things that I learned to
love?
Why must they die too?
-The Things I Learned to Love

Embracing her was like falling and trying to embrace the wind as it rushed all around me. I knew that eventually I would reach the ground and she would be gone, but for one perfect, blissful moment I felt as if I was flying.

 -*Wind*

Waking up is a silent war
Getting out of bed is an action
Of preposterous effort
I am my own worst enemy
I fight myself
Day in
And day out
Reluctant to look in the mirror
And meet my opponent
          -War

The book I always wanted to read
But could never write
Was about you
My love splayed out
Page after page after page
Of your name
Scrawled
In the ink of my bleeding heart
	-Scrawled

Willy arrives to find a stranger's car outside his
home
And all the hallways echoed with the sounds of
sighs and moans
His children say they hate him, they don't pay
him any mind
And his boss just laid him off because his work's
always behind

His car is making noises and it doesn't always
start
His breath's been labored lately so he's
concerned about his heart
While working on the sink last week he lost his
wedding ring
He shambles through a life that's full of small but
broken things

But every other Sunday around nine o'clock at
night
He moves into the basement and turns on all the
lights
Takes out all his brushes, pastels and pens in
black and gray
Then stands before a pallid canvas and paints it
all away

On one frigid winter evening he stood out in the
dark
And listened to the ache that had been swelling
in his heart
Deciding he knew what he had to do to end the
pain
He ate the muzzle of a gun and put a bullet
through his brain

Willy's wife remarried and put the old house up
for sale
Now his grave stands unadorned, all gloomy,
gray, and pale
The movers visited one day to clear out the estate
They went down to the basement so they could
gather up his things

They turned on all the lights and were soon filled
with surprise
As the apocalyptic scene they saw was seared
into their eyes
Every wall and room and corner was mercilessly
filled
With all the pain and joy and fear that Willy here
had spilled

The stains arrayed in black and gray had so
much in between

Worlds were curled within the walls like a
squandered inky dream
They lashed, they writhed, they lived, they died,
assailed from every side
They'll drag you down into the hell behind
Willy's icy eyes

     -A Portrait of the Artist as a Dead Man

There's a paper man inside me
He's a thin and fragile thing
Words punch holes in him
And he tears himself apart
He tries to fold himself
Into beautiful origami
A crane or rose
But he inevitably becomes unfurled
Unable to keep up the facade
And finds himself more wrinkled than before
  -Wrinkled

I'm sorry
To have worn a mask
And let you fall in love with it.
To have cursed you to love a character.
An act.
A false persona I invented
Because I thought the true me was unlovable.
Perhaps he his.
I think I too have learned to love my mask.
  -Unlovable

When standing in the light I have always chosen
To muse upon my own shadow
I run out of red paint and, rather than using
The millions of other pigments laid out before
me,
I tear open my wrists and paint a crimson sea of
sadness
I am an artist
And self-wrought tragedy is my muse
-I Am an Artist

Angels dress in black
To mourn the fact that God is dead
And it feels their celestial sadness
Has been poured inside my head
It trickles through my blood
And to the marrow of my bone
My heart begins to tear apart
As I hear their mournful tones
They sing a somber song
While they lay their king to rest
And as they sing I feel the sting
Of their heartbreak in my chest
                    -God is Dead

How does one win at this game of life?
Is death the finish line?
The way to win?
I have tried the shortest path to victory
By my own hand
I did not feel like a champion
It was not a gold medal
That I felt looped around my neck
Does one win by living?
That doesn't seem right either
Every day that I wake up
Feels like a loss
I'm tired of losing
I don't need to win
Just let me sit on the bench
Just for a moment
Catch my breath
Please let me stop
For a moment
        -Life

Depression is having a really sore neck.
It's not being able to look up and see the sun
Despite the fact
That I know it's *right* above me.
It's going to school
And making myself out of Play-Doh.
I mold myself into something
That's acceptable to the teacher.
That won't disturb the other students.
Something with a smile
And big clown shoes.
Something that sleeps at night.
And when I make these figurines
I always make sure to leave them hollow inside.
Depression is a clock that's 3 seconds fast.
It's always lying about itself.
Its life revolves around lying
And no one ever notices.
No one ever realizes the clock is off.
No one ever asks if the clock's okay.
No one ever tries to fix the clock.
And so it just keeps ticking
Always feeling slightly wrong.
　　　-Wrong

I kissed you at midnight
On New Years
One minute into the year
And my heart had already declared it
The best year yet
The same heart
That beats its steady rhythm
As I hold you in my arms
And as you rest your head on my shoulder
I wish to write you into some object
Some clichéd metaphor
But roses have thorns
And the stars are always out of reach
So I write you as you are
The love of my life

-Love of my Life

I don't think you could ever
See yourself
The way I see you
After all
It's in bad taste
To be hopelessly in love with yourself
I hope to be a mirror
To reflect the truest
And most loved image of you
I want you to look into me
Every morning
And feel unbroken
       -Mirror

My grandmother had a magic red coat
Every time I came over
She'd throw it on
Show her empty pockets
Then magically
Mysteriously
Like a rabbit from a hat
Pull candies from of nowhere
Tootsie rolls, peppermints, suckers
But soon the magic red coat disappeared
She exchanged it for a thin white gown
The candy became bitter
And her body became magic
She hired assistants in white coats
They helped her
Helped to pull from her magic body
Blood and IVs
Wires and tissue
And for her grand finale
With no warning
She made the light in her eyes
Disappear
Gone in an instant
I never knew
Where that light went
I hope it went somewhere good
A place where people wear red coats
Instead of white gowns

And the candy is never bitter
  -A Magic Red Coat

I belong to you
The way the moon
Belongs to the stars
Illuminating the world around it
Completing each other
And when the moon begins to wane
The stars continue to shine
Burning
Until their moon returns
Always waiting
Always there
When I wane
When I fade to crescent
And darkness creeps across me
The stars in your eyes
Will bring me back
And once again
I shall kiss the sky
-Kiss the Sky

I always face the wall when I sleep
But your bed is precisely in the center of the
room
Presenting a rather troubling paradox
So I always face away from you
Sometimes I feel guilty
When you pull me into your chest
And snuggle your face into the back of my neck
Breathing in my scent with every breath
I feel guilty
For showing my back to you
I never face you when we sleep
I'm afraid to see
Who closes their eyes first
       -When I Sleep

I have nothing to offer
But my empty hands
No riches and fame
No status
No more than you already have
But I offer myself and my empty hands
An emptiness so vast
It feels as if I have always been saving it
For someone like you
Someone filled with so much love
   -Empty Hands

Love in the sheets
Love in the way we stare at each other
Over our coffee mugs in the morning
Love in the way your dog tries to steal my kisses
Love in the way you mutter in your sleep at night
Responding to some surreal question
Or proposing some absurd postulate in your
dreams
And I pull you closer
And say

    Yes babe
    Whatever you just said
    Yes

Love in the precise way
You cross your arms behind my head
Every time you pull me in for a kiss
Love in the bedroom, in the kitchen,
On the sidewalk, in my heart
Everywhere love

      -Love

Lying in a boat
The wet seat cooly soaking into my shirt
As music floats from the speakers
And skips across the water
Frogs croak on the nearby shore
The moon glows above
Haloed by stars
One of them shoots
Or falls rather
And sinks below the horizon
Oh how I wish we could all just sink
     -Sink

A black umbrella
With aluminum bones
And a comfortable foam handle
I carry it with me everywhere
I block out the sunlight
I carry it
Unfurled on the street
Unfurled in my home
To hell with bad luck
I make my own darkness
        -Umbrella

If all the world's a stage
Then my life must be
Some kind of absurdist play
Some masterpiece of Ionesco or Beckett
It's confusing, funny, surprising
Entertaining at times
But in the end
Completely meaningless
    -Absurd

Find someone who loves your
Rough spots
Someone who treats your scars
Like the works of art they are
Who isn't afraid to cut themselves
On the broken parts of you
Who knows that it's not their job
To fix you
And accepts you as you are
  -Find Someone

I can't protect you from the world
I can't protect you from yourself
So cry if you must
But give me the privilege
Of holding you while you do
The world is cruel
So if you must cry
Never do it alone
Know your tears are always welcome
In my embrace

-Cry

I've lived my life in fear of silence
I've filled it with music
With TV
With the sound of fingers dancing across a
keyboard
Sometimes I turn on the fan
And face it towards the corner
Just to hear it spin
Trying to fill the silence
Anything to keep the world
From mirroring the emptiness inside me
      -Silence

I tear myself down
Bit by bit
Over and over
Hoping someday
To build myself into someone
Who can look into a mirror
And be okay
With the person on the other side
-The Other Side

She was the kind of girl
That the world fell in love with
Not the people in it
Though they fell for her too
But the world itself
The ground was always firm beneath her
The sun always a little brighter in her presence
And when she danced in the rain
Rather than becoming a wet mess like the rest of
us
She became beautiful
With her wet hair framing her face
And water dripping from her chin
And the stars in her eyes
        -The World Loved Her

I'm a flame
And you're gasoline
Amazing and beautiful on our own
I am warm and bright
Dancing in the wind
You are ancient and priceless
Nearly 3 fucking dollars a gallon
But together
What we create is so explosively beautiful
An eruption of heated passion
    -Together and Apart

May you be happy all your days.
May the main character
Live through every book you read.
And your favorite bands
Always sound like their first album.
I hope you always have an umbrella nearby
When it starts to rain.
And I pray your card
Never gets declined
In front of a line of gawking people
At the gas station.
May you live a life
Of small but happy things.

-Small but Happy Things

Like sand,
The more I tried to hold her
The more she slipped from my grasp
And scattered to the wind.
  -Sand

Like a crumbling building,
I must be torn down
In order to build myself back up.
Like a forest
On the brink of death,
I must burn
So that something beautiful
Can sprout from the ashes.

-Ashes

One day the phone rang
It warbled and sang
Calling and shouting for me
And I then felt the wind
That came chilling and killing
Old Eddie's Annabelle Lee
It chilled to the bone
And it cut to my soul
Compelling me onto my knees
And I desperately looked for
I desperately hoped for
An escape from this reality
But escape never came
And the news stayed the same
With no regard for my cries or my pleas
Now in every corner I look
Every cranny and nook
It's that cold, icy wind that I see
And I try to escape it
To evade it and run
But I know that it's coming for me
                -Chilling and Killing

You can't be depressed
You're smart
I've seen you play Trivia Crack
You're fucking good
You can't be depressed
You're in shape
Perhaps that's why I'm in shape
The constant "what ifs?"
The constant self hate
It's like cardio for my brain
You can't be depressed
You have friends
They love you
They only say they hate you when you're not
around
Or when you can't sleep at night
You can't be depressed
Dad doesn't hit you anymore
You can't be depressed
She's not dying anymore
She's been dead for years now
You don't have to watch her die
You can't be depressed
Because I don't want you to be depressed
It makes me sad
It's selfish of you to be depressed and make me
sad

-Selfish

There's nothing back at home
I left behind all the things I didn't need
My friends, my dog, my family
And all the broken parts of me
They say there's no place like home
And I think they may be right
I've never seen a place so full of tears
So full of sad and lonely nights
Now I live life on the road
I've seen so many faces on my way
I've seen pretty ones and tearstained ones
I see them every day
I've seen faces like the mountains
Cracked with jagged lines
And I've seen faces that have yet to crack
They'll erode away with time
I've seen the faces of the women
That left me lusting in their wake
Faces beautifully composed
Invitations to heartache
And every day I see a face I hate
A face I loathe to greet
I see him in the morning
Every time I brush my teeth
-Faces

The boys went off to war again
Hoping to return as men
The girls now wives
Will dry their eyes
And look upon the horizon
Mother will sit within her home
And hope her son is not alone
Send prayers out on silent tears
Prayers that will never reach their ears
Their ears are filled with shots and screams
And all manner of such hellish things
The sounds will move into their heads
Take residence until they're dead
And all her prayers will come true
Granted by the gods she knew
She'll see it when her son comes home
She'll know he'll never be alone
Because all the dark and death and dread
Upon the warfront that he met
Will be with him until he's dead
Inside his heart
Inside his head
      -Inside His Head

He roamed the hallways
Passing from classroom to classroom
The fluorescent lights seemed dim
Perhaps because his head was always bowed
At each class he stopped
Outside the door
Breathed deeply
Stepped inside
Murmured to the teacher
Motioned for a student to follow
Back to his office
Back to his desk
And he talked
Talked of the singular absence
That permeated every class
Every heart
And the tears flowed
Flowed like students in the hallway
At the end of the day
Rushing to get out
Tears for the classmate
The lab partner
The friend
He lets them return to their classes
Firmly
With a handshake, a pat, a hug
And now it's just him
And the desk

And the tears
The bell rings
The students begin to flow
So too the tears
Dripping
Staining
The desk of the wounded healer
   -Wounded Healer

I remember it well
Our three dogs
Two cats
Every square inch of every room
Every blade of grass of all three acres
The shitty carpet on the stairs
The shittier carpet on the landing
The fist shaped hole
In dad's bedroom door
That shouted at me
Every time I walked past
The smaller fist shaped hole
In the wall of my room
That weakly shouted back
The fireplace
That was perpetually dirty
Despite never being used
The family room
That perpetually lacked a family
The tree where I felt less alone
Until the branch snapped
And like a cartoon
Where the character floats weightlessly
Until they look down
And then drop to the center of the earth
I fell

    -I Remember

She was a master craftswoman
She had suffered so much heartache
So much loss
Life had taken away all the good
And exchanged it for tearstained pillows
Despite that
She takes her loss and heartache
She holds it in the palm of her hand
Gently
And crafts from it a beautiful life
   -*A Beautiful Life*

I could see it in others when I looked at them. They were different. When they looked at the world around them, at life, they saw opportunity and fun and happiness. However, when I looked around I saw only darkness. Rather than what was or what could be, I saw only what could have been. And I found myself saddened, because what could have been was so much more beautiful.

-What Could Have Been

I see the gray marble
Of your headstone
In my eyes
And the impending shadow
Of your death
In my dark hair
My existence is a reminder
That you will one day die
-Memento Mori

I want the world to know our love
Fuck a barbaric yawp
I want an ecstatic declaration
Of my devotion to you
I want to wear my heart
On your sleeve
        -Sleeve

Like the fruit of the tree of knowledge
I long to taste you
Though I am told it is wrong
I long to hold you
To know your sweetness
Damn the people
Damn God
Damn him to hell
I will have you
My love
                 -Forbidden Fruit

I used to do math in my head during mass
The priest would stand at his pulpit
And preach our salvation
Or our damnation
And I would be there
Multiplying two by two by two
And on and on and on
Until the number became so big
It spilled from my head
And so I'd start over again
I would intentionally mispronounce the words in
the hymnals
A subtle form of blasphemy
A slight dissonance in the voices of the choir
I refused to accept religion
I refused to accept anything greater than me
Nothing had ever brought me praying to my
knees
Until the day I met you
I have been a believer ever since

-Church

I used to think
I couldn't be happy
I'd imagine scenario
After scenario
After scenario
Attempting to find
What would bring me peace
A little money here
A nice house there
Moving to a better climate
A job I don't hate
But nonetheless
At the end of those scenarios
I was never happy
I realize now
That I never accounted for
Meeting you
              -Scenarios

This house is built on sadness
Bricks made of regret
Its mortar of mistakes
Its brittle bones of sleepless nights
Blood leaks forth as saline tears
Pumping
Broken hearts still pumping
The two halves of this house's heart
Now sleep in separate rooms
    -This House

Holden Caulfield stands on a ledge
Looking down at the ground below
Wishing to yank the earth up toward him
At approximately 9.8 meters per second per
second
All the while Raskolnikov wanders boulevards
As an axe knocks against his side
Knock
Knock
Knock
Searching for an escape
Gatsby stares across the moat
The world becomes green
Green world, green light, green paper
Green can buy love
And John
Good old Savage John
He's swinging in the doorframe
Knock
Knock
Knock
His therapist always disapproved
Of his refusal to take his Soma
Around the walls Hector is dragged
Flesh torn from sinew
Sinew torn from bones
On the rampart King Hamlet walks
In his purgatory

He reaches the prince's door
Knock
Knock
Knock
Nobody answers
Such is the tragedy of life
Such is the tragedy of death
-Such is the Tragedy

You are the face
That launched a thousand ships
And broke a thousand hearts
Your lips upon my neck
Your body in my arms
The warmth of you
Like fire in the snow
Of cold sheets
Like two trees
Planted atop each other
We lie intertwined
Our bodies entangled
Wrapped up in our heartstrings
    -Heartstrings

I grasped after your fleeting shadow
And though I have lived my entire life shunning
the light
It was a darkness
I could never quite embrace
And so you left
And in your absence
The shadows seemed to grow longer in the
morning
And even longer in the evening
In the absence of the light
They all became your shadow
A shadow I have lived in ever since
    -Shadows

Does time pass more slowly
During the good times
And more quickly
During the bad times
When you wear an expensive watch?
Do the mountains become less steep
And the valleys less deep
Depending on the brand of your shoes?
Would you love my touch more
If my hands weren't so callused?
-Calluses

Choke down my dose of waking up
It's a sweet and bitter kind of drug
The world is cold despite the sun
And I just want to sleep
I hear the world has a lovely glow
I only see the shadows though
When I look at all this art
I simply see the darkest parts
I think I'm in love with the dark
And I'm too afraid to break its heart
So I hide the bruises
And claim that I fell down the stairs
Anything to stay in the dark
Although the dark has never cared
    -*Bitter Drug*

I set fire to my world
Just to burn the dark away.
And quench it with the clouds
That stop to pour one out
For the friends who fade too soon.
The tears of thunderheads
Roll down my cheeks
And drown me in my sorrow.
In my endless self pity.
The saddest book I ever read
Had a mirror at the end.

-Burning the Dark

I didn't know I was alive
Until the day I met your eyes
And all the world began to shine
With possibility
The sky was something new
It became a shining sapphire blue
With hints of cobalt showing through
And it's all because of you
The roses lost their teeth and thorns
The devil lost his baleful horns
My heart began to swoop and soar
With every glimpse of you
And all the nights were turned to day
The dark abyss was chased away
Your golden glow was here to stay
As my arms encircled you
-*The Day We Met*

You say I deserve the world,
But you are my world.
So I'll settle for you
And only you.
     -*You*

I'm not good at staying home alone
And I'm not good at going out
I live life in between
In a state of constantly wanting my bed
And a constant fear of missing out
When I leave this room I'm a ghost
Wandering through the streets
Empty eyed and empty souled
Too afraid to remain in the grave
Too afraid to go out into the world
Transparent and empty
Not quite there
Never quite anywhere
Always drifting in between life and death
-Everything in Between

Love your scars.
They will stay with you forever.
They are daily reminders
Of all the things you have survived
And all the things
That didn't survive you.
      -Reminders

I kiss you with my eyes open
I fear that if I don't
When I pull away and look
You'll be gone
Just a stolen kiss
And
Nothing
-Nothing

Your past doesn't make you
Any less beautiful
Or any less worthy
All that pain and loss
Only strengthens you
A geode must be broken
Before its crystals can shine through

   -Crystals

Become a storm
That can douse the blazes
Of negativity
Shine like lightning
Rumble like thunder
Be so fearsome
That people will stand outside their homes
And watch in awe
As you approach
　　　-Storm

I hold my cold heart in my hands
And try to keep it warm for you
So when I find you
Or your love finds me
It will be easy to hold
And I won't have to fear
You returning it
And leaving me for a warmer heart
  -Cold Heart

Sometimes we must fall
Before we can rise
Die before we can live
Like seeds
That must be planted in graves
Before they can bloom
We too must bury ourselves
Beneath the weight of everything
Only to push through
And grow

    -Seeds

Some things exist only
To be experienced
To be felt deep inside the chest
Somewhere more important than the heart
So I don't wish to understand you
Only to feel you
And know you
Within me

     -Understanding

I've lived a life half full
Every woman half loved
Every crossword incomplete
Every game of chess
Ends with the pieces at my feet
And I only enjoy my days
Until the sun reaches high noon
My nights are only peaceful
Before the sky is crested by the moon
Summer is too hot
And winter far too cold
Fall and spring are the only times
When the weather seems controlled
And the only times that I'm alive
Or I feel that I'm okay
Is when I put my pen to paper
And shut the world away
      -Half Full

As someone who's always been alone
My dearest friends, you are my home
A place to roost, a bed to rest
And perpetual permission to lay my head upon
your chest
An ocean of shoulders to absorb my tears
And all your gentle voices to allay my nagging
fears
You are where I go when the world is too obscene
And when knocked onto my knees you are the
rock on which I lean
As long as I have you all, I shall never roam
Because I'll love you always, and love's what
makes a home
     -Hymn to my Friends

Of all the women I've been with
Of all the women I decided
I could die for
You are the one I chose to live for
And that has always been the hardest thing
-I'd Die for You

Such is your beauty
That the stars flicker
And dim
When you walk beneath them
    -Flicker

I am torn by two opposing forces: the desperate need to be loved, and the penetrating guilt at having allowed someone such as myself to be loved by another. Such is my life. A constant battle between some void inside me that needs to be filled and the knowledge that I am poison.

-Poison

I look at things through hollow, glassy eyes
Empty
Like a landscape painted by a painter
With no soul
The birds plastered lifeless, flightless all across
the sky
The river is a cold icy snake dividing the canvas
And all the grass and trees are but weeds left
unkempt
I've stared at these lifeless things
With lifeless eyes
And seen a mirror
       -Lifeless

Every day with you is a lifetime
An ocean within a bucket
61 seconds in a minute
Far too easily
I become lost in the eternity of your smile
    -Eternity

Distance keeps the hope away
As we dance
One step forward
And two steps back
And I know that you're afraid of me
Afraid of codependency
But please just hold my hand
As the world burns down around us
      -Distance

Inside me there is a flame
I've stoked to life
That bears your name
It keeps me dry
It keeps me warm
It lights the way
Through every storm
Thought it may grow cold
And dim within my soul
I'll bring it back to life
And bathe in it's loving glow
    -Flame

Let me paint over your scars
With the blush of love
And turn your tears
To beads of sweat
That roll down your
Lithe
Ready
Body
As we dance
In between the sheets
        -Paint

I don't know how to convince you
That I'm not like the others
You've been hurt so many times
That their faces have all blurred into one
And this blur is all you see when you look at me
I move too slow
And you fear that my feelings aren't real
I move too fast
And you fear that I'm using you
I merely want to hold you
To carry you in my arms
Bringing you to a world without pain
And let all the weight of past mistakes
Wash away
-Hurt

Down my cheeks the tears will dry
As I think upon my life
And all the things I forgot to love
Quiet in our bed at night
I'll wallow in my mental strife
And wonder at what exists above
And in these times of moral plight
I'll pull you close and hold you tight
My never ending love
     -The Tears Will Dry

I was hers to do with
As she pleased
A blank block of wood
Covered in old knots and scars
And I gave her a blade
To whittle me into
What I was always meant to be
And hoped that she'd be happy
With the person she had formed
      -*Shapes*

My life is a game of Russian Roulette
I wake up every morning
Wondering if today is the chamber with the
bullet in it
If today I pull the trigger
And there are no more tomorrows
My life is the riskiest of games
A game that revolves around not knowing
I think the not knowing is the only reason
I keep waking up
I never liked unanswered questions
  -Russian Roulette

In this world there are only those who are in love and those who are searching. I'm afraid I've become lost somewhere in between.

   -Lost

More than just physically beautiful
She was enticing in both mind and spirit
A burning star of immeasurable gravity
That shared with everyone its light and warmth
     -Gravity

When speaking of friends gone before
You talk in present tense
because their ghosts are living in your mind
The phantoms you invent
These specters you let loose every time a loved
one dies
Because you never said goodbye
They stare at you from every mirror and every
polished spoon
Visiting you night by night just like the nightly
moon
The moon lights up the dark and bathes you in
its glow
But these spirits only bring you sadness, tears,
and woe
    -Spirits

The walls are all painted in funeral colors
The world is cast in shades of gray and blue
A life destined to fail and suffer
The only life I ever knew
Please just let me see some other
A dash of yellow, a shade of red
Within these somber shades I'm smothered
They've begun to leak into my head
        -*Colors*

You were always unique
And a particularly hard worker
So I like to think that you're buried seven feet
underground
And just like in life
That little bit of uniqueness
That small amount of extra work
That one extra foot
Makes me feel infinitely further from you
    -Seven Feet Under

I am an old and weary home
My roof sags beneath the weight of many years
Shrubs and grass grow wildly out front
Splayed hands reaching desperately for
something
Here you'll see my foundation is broken
Damage done long ago when I was just a boy
Being built into a man
And here my doors screech
Shuddering on their rusted hinges
As you try to pull them open
I have learned to be wary of letting people in
The upstairs is labyrinthian
The same dark paths looping in on themselves
A part of me I never learned to navigate
And deep down
At the core of this decrepit structure
Is a hearth that has gone cold

-Home

I long for the love of the necromancer
Deep, dark, sultry love
Love that will bring me peace
Love that will revive
That small part of me
That died long ago
-Necromancer

I sought money and power
Success in all its various forms
Academics and social prestige
I always thought that would make me happy
I thought success would fix me
But now I've learned
That all I ever needed
Was you
And that look in your eyes
When you're nestled in my arms
   -All I Need

I cast a shadow and I hate myself for it. It's silly, I realize. After all, one can't stand in the light without also casting a shadow. Nonetheless, I hated the shadow for the necessity of its existence.

-Necessity

Endings are sad
That's why I cry at sunsets
And checkmates
And funerals
And the end of American Idol
But I've recently discovered
That all endings are also beginnings
And vice versa
So now I cry at beginnings too
   -Endings

If you enjoyed this, consider supporting me in the following ways:

Follow Me:
Instagram: @authortravisliebert
Tumblr: @authortravisliebert

Check out my other books
This is Death, Love, Life
Perchance to Dream

<u>A special look at *This is Death, Love, Life*</u>

We wage wars inside our minds
Silent fights behind our eyes
Maimed by words unkindly said
Tamed by our prescription meds
But trudging on with all our might
We veterans of silent fights
Hope that we'll see better days
As long as we attempt to stay
Alive

   -Alive

I remember that foul morning
When they interrupted class
And in a voice replete with mourning
Said you were never coming back
I stood out in the hallway
And watched our English teacher cry
We ate in silence that day
We never thought you'd die
It always is so horrid
The passing of a youth
So depressing, sad, and morbid
A cruel and somber truth
I can't believe you're gone
You've left wounds I'll never mend
But I'll bear my scars and continue on
Rest in peace my friend

-My Friend

She was a rose
Who wilted
Waiting for one
Who dared to grasp her thorns

-Rose

We venture out into the world
And assume our shameful daily task
Of fearing what our peers might think
And putting on a public mask
Smothering our private passions
Behind our masks we suffocate
And watch as others do the same
Letting their dreams asphyxiate

-Masks

About the Author

Lauded as a "pretty nice guy" by his peers, Travis Liebert is a native of Louisville, Kentucky and a member of the widely invasive species "Homo sapiens sapiens." His hobbies include reading, writing, and anything else that indicates he's intelligent and literate. He went to Trinity High School where he openly brandished his stunning repertoire of useless knowledge as captain of the quick recall team. He is now a perpetually absent student at the University of Louisville. *Everything in Between* is his third poetry collection.